PRAYERS FOR LIFE

"Two kinds of truth merge within this book: the truths of modern science that reveal the amazing development of a child in the womb, and the truth of faith expressed in prayer. As offered in this book, both truths evoke love: love for God, to whom we pray, and love for each child forming in a mother's womb, for whom we pray. May this book help you to foster the growth of both loves."

Rev. Mitch Pacwa, S.J
Host of *EWTN Live*

"Mary Ann Kuharski beautifully reminds us that all of our actions to preserve life must be focused on Christ and rooted in prayer. This is a wonderful resource for individuals and pro-life groups of all kinds."

Joseph M. Scheidler
National Director, Pro-Life Action League

"This book is a wonderful treasure for the pro-life movement. The powerful reflections and prayers combine beautifully to encourage a deeper commitment to life at every stage."

Rev. Bill Miscamble, C.S.C.
Founding President, Notre Dame Faculty for Life

"There are few in the pro-life movement as dedicated, passionate, and experienced as Mary Ann Kuharski. Nationally known speaker and author, and founder of PROLIFE Across AMERICA, Mary Ann has lived and breathed the pro-life cause for many years. Her billboards are like sentinels standing on our highways and byways, reminding us of the preciousness of human life. *Prayers for Life* is a pro-life prayer book containing forty daily meditations. The book is simple, yet thought provoking, and draws the reader into prayer for human life from conception onward. The fruit of Kuharski's many years of praying for human life, *Prayers for Life* is founded on quotations from the scriptures, which set the theme for each reflection. It also contains significant quotations from popes, priests, saints, and lay people among others. It contains, as well, inspiring factual statements on human life in the womb. All this in a simple-to-follow daily format. I highly recommend *Prayers for Life*. It is a valuable resource and a significant contribution to the building up of a culture of life through prayer."

Most Reverend John M. LeVoir
Bishop of New Ulm

PRAYERS FOR LIFE

Forty Daily Devotions

MARY ANN KUHARSKI

ave maria press AmP notre dame, indiana

Nihil Obstat: Rev. Joseph R. Johnson
                Censor librorum

Imprimatur: Most Rev. John C. Nienstedt
               Archbishop of St. Paul and Minneapolis
               July 18, 2013

Founded in 1865, Ave Maria Press is a ministry of the United States Province of Holy Cross.

www.avemariapress.com

Paperback ISBN-13 978-1-59471-419-1

E-Book ISBN-13 978-1-59471-420-7

Cover image © Christie's Images Ltd./SuperStock.

Cover and text design by Andy Wagoner.

Printed and bound in the United States of America.

Library of Congress Cataloging-in-Publication Data
Kuharski, Mary Ann.
 Prayers for life : forty daily devotions / Mary Ann Kuharski.
    pages cm
 Summary: "Provides an inspiring forty-day devotional ideal for anyone concerned about abortion and the dignity of life"-- Provided by publisher.
  ISBN 978-1-59471-419-1 -- ISBN 978-1-59471-420-7
1. Life--Religious aspects--Christianity. 2. Life--Religious aspects--Catholic Church. 3. Right to life. 4. Catholic Church--Prayers and devotions. I. Title.
 BT696.K84 2014
 248.4--dc23
                          2013033167

To my loving husband, John, and our beautiful children: Chrissy, Timmy, Charlie, Tina, Tony, Theresa, Vincent, Mary, Angie, Kari, Michael, Dominic, and Joseph (who will be ordained a priest on May 31, 2014).

This book is offered as a special thanksgiving to those from our own era who have spoken and worked valiantly for the cause of life—including Blessed Pope John Paul II, Blessed Mother Teresa of Calcutta, and Venerable Archbishop Fulton J. Sheen (whose television and radio programs inspired me in my youth).

God Bless You!
Mary R. Kraus
4-8-14

Rejoice in hope, be patient under trial, persevere in prayer.

—Romans 12:11–12

Eye has not seen, ear has not heard, nor has it so much as dawned on man what God has prepared for those who love him.

—1 Corinthians 2:9–10 (NAB)

Dear Lord, help us to be your Ambassadors of faith and life to all those we meet in our everyday lives. You made each of us in your image and likeness and want us to be happy with you for all eternity. Help us by our words and deeds to share that joy with others and always to keep in mind that our number-one goal in life is not fame, success, or wealth, but everlasting happiness with you in heaven.

Introduction

When the Supreme Court announced its decision in the *Roe v. Wade* case on January 22, 1973, many opinion makers and news commentators in the dominant secular media predicted that abortion would be a "nonissue" within five years. But thanks to people of faith and pro-lifers across the nation, the issue of abortion in America has continued to be prominent in every campaign and election—on a local and a national level. The reason is simple—legal abortion involves the direct killing of an innocent baby in the womb. It also is an abandonment of a mother, perhaps in her time of greatest need.

Since the 1973 decision, more than 1.3 million unborn babies have died each year. Most are tiny in size, yet they have a beating heart as early as eighteen days from conception and brain waves that can be detected as early as forty-two days. Other babies aborted in the later months of pregnancy are fully developed and large enough to be held in a hand or cradled in an adult's arms. The only crime they have in common is being unwanted, imperfect, or inconvenient.

It is almost impossible to imagine: More than 1.3 million babies die each year. In his encyclical *The Gospel of Life*,

Blessed Pope John Paul II declares this situation a "culture of death." And that is what it is.

Techniques, once perfected to save pre-born babies, are now routinely used to test these babies for Down syndrome, spina bifida, or other maladies; and when there is even a slight possibility of these maladies being found, expectant mothers are encouraged to "terminate the pregnancy" (a more polite phrase than "dismember and destroy a living, breathing infant in the womb"). Some babies are aborted merely because they are seen as being the wrong sex.

On the other end of life's spectrum, health care for the elderly, infirm, and chronically ill is now being weighed against the cost and even inconvenience to the family. A growing number of states are proposing legislation allowing mercy killing or euthanasia. Oregon was the first to pass such a law.

In spite of this culture-of-death mentality that permeates society, there is growing evidence of a return to a culture of life. The following are a few examples:

Young people—teens and young adults—are swelling the ranks of the pro-life movement. Rejecting the pro-abortion propaganda of the pleasure seeking and self-indulgent, young people not only are appearing at marches and pro-life rallies, but their voices are being heard in legislatures and in the halls of Congress. Armed with a sense of faith and a fundamental belief in the sacredness of human life, they are a force to be reckoned with.

Recent polls, including those by the dominant secular media, are showing a shift to the pro-life position, as more and more citizens are repulsed by the sheer ugliness of abortion—most especially late-term and partial-birth abortion.

Post-abortion women as well as men, who were once involved in abortion or its advocacy, are joining the pro-life movement in great numbers. Their voices and testimonies of their own devastating experiences with abortion cannot be ignored. They know the truth, and the truth has set them free (see Jn 8:32).

Lastly, and most importantly, millions of pro-life people hold an abiding and deep faith that cannot be undermined or shaken. It is that faith and trust that gives them joy in the midst of this culture of death.

Prayers for Life is offered as a small tool to those pro-lifers in the trenches, whether praying in front of an abortion clinic, offering assistance to those experiencing an untimely pregnancy, counseling those recovering from a previous abortion, caring for an elderly parent, or visiting the sick, shut-ins, or the imprisoned.

Let us pray together and share our mutual faith and love of Jesus Christ. Let us spread our joy to all we meet—including those who do not share our faith or fundamental values. And let us be encouraged and inspired by the saints of the past, as well as the holy men and women of our own times, such as Blessed Pope John Paul II, Venerable Archbishop Fulton J. Sheen, Blessed Mother Teresa of Calcutta, Pope Benedict XVI, and Pope Francis.

> Rejoice in the Lord, not in the world. That is, rejoice in the truth, not in wickedness; rejoice in the hope of eternity, not in the fading flower of vanity. . . . Wherever you are on earth, however long you remain on earth, the Lord is near. Do not be anxious about anything. (St. Augustine)

For All Mothers

Can a mother forget her infant,
be without tenderness for the child of her womb?
Even should she forget, I will never forget you.
See, upon the palms of my hands
I have written your name.

—Isaiah 49:15–16 (NAB)

Reflection

- "The most important person on earth is a mother. She cannot claim the honor of having built the Notre Dame cathedral. She need not. She has built something more magnificent than any cathedral—a dwelling for an immortal soul, the tiny perfection of her baby's body. The angels have not been blessed with such a grace. They cannot share in God's creative miracle to bring new saints to Heaven. Only a human mother can. Mothers are closer to God the Creator than any other creature. God joins forces with mothers in performing this act of creation. . . . What on God's good earth

1

is more glorious than this: to be a mother?" (Joseph
Cardinal Mindszenty).

- In his book *Crossing the Threshold of Hope*, Blessed Pope
  John Paul II encourages, "Do not be afraid of being
  witnesses to the dignity of every human, from the
  moment of conception."
- "The Lord called me from birth, from my mother's
  womb he gave me my name" (Is 49:1).

Life begins at conception. A new individual receives
twenty-three chromosomes from each parent. He or she
is truly a unique individual human being, never to be
repeated. Once fertilization has taken place, ovum and
sperm no longer exist. A new person has been created.
At this stage this new person is a tiny living organism
weighing only 15 ten-millionths of a gram.

Let Us Pray

Heavenly Father, we know that in your eyes there is no
such thing as an unwanted child. While some babies may
be a "surprise" in the eyes of the world, you have a plan
and a purpose for *each* one. Please help us to be people
of joy, rejoicing at the gift of each new little one (*fetus* in
Latin)—a gentle witness that *all* human life is sacred and
created by God who makes no mistakes. Amen.

You Are the Light of the World

You are the light of the world. A city set on a mountain cannot be hidden. Nor do they light a lamp and then put it under a bushel basket. They set it on a lampstand where it gives light to all in the house. Just so, your light must shine before others so that they may see your good deeds and glorify your heavenly Father.

—Matthew 5:14–16

Reflection

- St. Teresa of Avila urges, "We ought to make some progress, however little, every day, and show some increase of fervor. We ought to act as if we were at war—as, indeed, we are—and never relax until we have won victory."

- If we're unsure what God is calling us to do, Blessed John Henry Cardinal Newman reminds us that "God has created me to do Him some definite service; He has committed some work to me which He has not committed to another. I have my mission—I may never know it in this life but I shall be told it in the next."

- To be sure, St. Teresa tells us, "You pay God a compliment by asking great things of Him."

- "So we are ambassadors for Christ, as if God were appealing through us" (2 Cor 5:20).

At the moment of conception/fertilization, all the necessary elements that create a new human being are present. When the chromosomes of the father and mother unite, they form an absolutely unique, never-to-be-duplicated human person. At that moment, life begins. From that moment on, any further formation of the person is purely a matter of development, growth, and maturation. From the moment of conception the child grows. And the child keeps growing until life ends.

Let Us Pray

Dear Lord, help us to be your light of faith and life in this culture of death that surrounds us. Grant us courage mixed with gentleness as we strive to be a witness to others—whether members of our family, our community, or those we meet in the workplace and the world in which we live. Help us to be your Ambassadors for life to every-one we meet this day. Amen.

Knit in My Mother's Womb

You formed my inmost being;
you knit me in my mother's womb.
I praise you, because I am wonderfully made;
wonderful are your works.

—Psalm 139:13–14

Reflection

- St. Vincent de Paul reminds us, "Let us stop saying, 'It is I who have done this work.' For every good thing ought to be done in the name of our Lord Jesus Christ."

- "Lord, you have probed me, you know me; you know when I sit and when I stand; you understand my thoughts from afar" (Ps 139:1–2).

- "The Lord is your guardian; the Lord is your shade at your right hand. By day the sun will not strike you, nor the moon by night. The Lord will guard you from all evil" (Ps 121:5–7).

On the first day of new life, the first cell divides into two, the two into four, and so on. Each of these new cells divides again and again as they travel toward the womb in search of a protected place to grow.

Let Us Pray

Heavenly Father, help us always to advocate for the most vulnerable in our midst—from the unborn threatened by abortion; to the mother in poverty or fear; to the elderly, weak, or infirm. We lift up in prayer, too, those who are the *forgotten*, those unable or unwilling to pray, and those who do not know you. Help them to see you in others and to recognize your merciful and unconditional love.

Help us to be people of faith and to radiate your love and compassion to all others. And help us to remember too, that the good we do is not our own doing but is from *you*. Amen.

Hear the Orphan's Plea

Make justice your aim; redress the wronged,
hear the orphan's plea, defend the widow.

—Isaiah 1:17

Reflection

- Blessed Pope John Paul II challenges us:
  We will stand up every time that human life is
  threatened.

  When the sacredness of life before birth is
  attacked, we will stand up and proclaim that no
  one ever has the authority to destroy unborn life.

  When a child is described as a burden or looked
  upon only as a means to satisfy an emotional
  need, we will stand up and insist that every child
  is a unique and unrepeatable gift of God, with the
  right to a loving and united family. . . .

  When the sick, the aged or the dying are
  abandoned in loneliness, we will stand up and
  proclaim that they are worthy of love, care and

respect. (John Paul II, "Homily," Mass at the Capital Mall, October 7, 1979, 6)

- St. Ignatius of Loyola instructs, "Let us work as if success depends on us alone, but with heartfelt conviction that we are doing nothing and God everything."

- "Then you will again see the distinction between the just and the wicked; between him who serves God, and him who does not serve him. For lo, the day is coming, blazing like an oven, when all the proud and all the evildoers will be stubble" (Mal 3:18–19 NAB).

By eighteen days from conception, the heart begins to beat with the baby's own blood, often a different type from the mother's. This is a unique human being.

Let Us Pray

Dear Lord, please instill in our hearts the message of love you so freely gave through your divine Son. Help us never to tire or weaken in our goal to defend and protect all human life, from the very youngest to the oldest and most vulnerable. Help us to see you in everyone and to treat all people—including those who oppose us—with kindness and love. Amen.

For the Children in Our Midst

Taking a child, he placed it in their midst, and putting his arms around it he said to them, "Whoever receives one child such as this in my name, receives me; and whoever receives me, receives not me, but the One who sent me."

—Mark 9:36–37

Reflection

- Blessed Pope John Paul II tells us, "A person who believes in the essential goodness of all creation is capable of discovering all the secrets of creation, in order to perfect continually the work assigned to him by God."

- St. Augustine of Hippo observes, "God loves each of us as if there were only one of us."

- "Do not be afraid of those who kill the body but cannot kill the soul; rather, be afraid of the one who can destroy both soul and body in Gehenna. Are not two sparrows sold for a small coin? Yet not one of them falls to the ground without your Father's knowledge. Even all the hairs of your head are counted. So do not be afraid; you are worth more than many sparrows" (Mt 10:28–31).

By twenty-eight days from conception, a baby has eyes, ears, and even a tongue.

Let Us Pray

Dear Lord Jesus, help all of us involved in this great movement for life to never waver in rejoicing at the gift of new life. We pray that we may see *all* others as your precious children—even those who oppose us or appear hostile. Help us to pray for those in our midst who may be starving—not for food—but for you. Help us to see even those who are, as Blessed Mother Teresa of Calcutta says, "Jesus appearing in distressing disguise," and treat them with love.

Help us, Lord, to be joyful people who radiate truth as we recognize the beauty and wonder of your creation—from the tiniest snowflake, to the sprouting of springtime buds, to the infant in the womb—and to carry that joy to all those we meet this day. Amen.

The Healing Touch of Kindness

You listen, Lord, to the needs of the poor;
you strengthen their heart and incline your ear.
You win justice for the orphaned and oppressed.

—Psalm 10:17–18

Reflection

- Who in my midst needs my help? Is there someone I may be overlooking in my "busy-ness?" Is there someone craving my time, yearning for attention, a listening ear, a consoling heart? Is there someone in need of a refreshing cup of *my* love?

- St. Catherine of Siena prays: "My Lord, what do you want me to do? I will do it."

- "After this, there was a feast of the Jews, and Jesus went up to Jerusalem. Now there is in Jerusalem at the Sheep [Gate] a pool called in Hebrew Bethesda, with five porticoes. In these lay a large number of ill, blind, lame and crippled. One man was there who had been ill for thirty-eight years. When Jesus saw him lying there and knew that he had been ill for a long time, he said to him, 'Do you want to be well?' The sick man answered him, 'Sir, I have no one to put me into the pool when the water is stirred up; while I am on my way, someone else gets down there before me.' Jesus said to him, 'Rise, take up your mat and walk.' Immediately the man became well, took up his mat, and walked" (Jn 5:1–9).

At twenty-eight days from conception, muscles are developing along the future spine. Arms and legs are budding.

Let Us Pray

Dear Lord, help me to respond to the needs of others. Teach me patience and give me the kindness and the gentleness of your mother to see those in need, not through my eyes, but yours. Help me to touch and love as you would. And when sickness or pain comes to me, help me to see it as a *gift* to offer you, and in the words of St. Francis de Sales, "Make sickness itself a prayer." Amen.

The Infant Leaped in Her Womb

When Elizabeth heard Mary's greeting, the infant leaped in her womb, and Elizabeth, filled with the Holy Spirit, cried out in a loud voice and said: "Most blessed are you among women and blessed is the fruit of your womb."

—Luke 1:41–42

Reflection

- St. Teresa of Avila wrote a poem expressing her desire to be what God wanted her to be:

  > I am yours and born for you,
  > What do you want of me?
  > Majestic sovereign,
  > Unending wisdom,
  > Kindness pleasing to my soul;
  > God sublime, one being good,
  > Yours, you made me,

> Yours, you saved me,
> Yours, you endured me,
> Yours, you called me
> Yours, you awaited me,
> Yours, I did not stray.
> What do You want of me?

- St. Edith Stein (a Jewish convert to Catholicism who was martyred in a Nazi concentration camp) writes of truth, "Whenever you seek truth, you seek God, whether or not you know it."

- "Before I formed you in the womb I knew you; before you were born I dedicated you" (Jer 1:5).

By thirty days from conception, the child has grown ten thousand times and is now six to seven millimeters (one-quarter inch) long. The brain has human proportions. Blood flows in the veins (but stays separate from mother's blood).

Let Us Pray

Heavenly Father, St. John the Baptist was the herald who proclaimed the coming of Christ—even before birth! He leaped for joy at the presence of Mary and Jesus within her. Help us, Lord, to always be people of joy, no matter the obstacles, and to proclaim the truth, the beauty, and the sacredness of *all* human life—born and unborn.

Help us never to tire in our commitment to life and always offer assistance to those in need. May we be, as St. Paul says, your Ambassadors for truth and life in whatever circumstance we find ourselves. Grant this through our Lord Jesus Christ, your Son, who lives and reigns with you and the Holy Spirit, one God now and forever. Amen.

DAY EIGHT

Weep for Our Children

Jesus turned to them and said, "Daughters of Jerusalem, do not weep for me; weep instead for yourselves and for your children, for indeed, the days are coming when people will say, 'Blessed are the barren, the wombs that never bore, and the breasts that never nursed.'"

—Luke 23:28–29

Reflection

• Blessed Mother Teresa of Calcutta spoke out often in defense of the unborn and against abortion. She explains, "God has invested all his love in creating human life. That is why we are not entitled to destroy it, especially we who know that Christ has died for the salvation of that life. Christ has died and has given everything for that child."

Outspoken and unwavering in her commitment to the downtrodden and those most in need, born and unborn, Blessed Mother Teresa did not hesitate to remind even leaders of nations about the scourge of abortion. She spoke of it when receiving the Nobel Peace Prize and when addressing the National Prayer Breakfast in Washington, DC. Her message was eloquent and clear in defense of *all* human life!

- St. Elizabeth Ann Seton urges, "We must pray literally without ceasing—without ceasing in every occurrence and employment of our lives. You know I mean that prayer of the heart which is independent of place or situation, or which is, rather, a habit of lifting up the heart to God, as in a constant communication with Him."

- "Just one thing: forgetting what lies behind but straining forward to what lies ahead, I continue my pursuit toward the goal, the prize of God's upward calling, in Christ Jesus" (Phil 3:13–14).

By forty-two days from conception, the skeleton is formed. The brain coordinates movement of muscles and organs. Reflex responses have begun.

Let Us Pray

Heavenly Father, send down your Holy Spirit to guide us. Give us your grace and the courage to be tireless advocates for the most vulnerable and defenseless. Help us to be as unrelenting as Blessed Mother Teresa and pray without ceasing. Amen.

Pray for Your Persecutors

You have heard that it was said, "You shall love your neighbor and hate your enemy." But I say to you, love your enemies and pray for those who persecute you that you may be children of your heavenly Father.

—Matthew 5:43–45

Reflection

- St. Angela Merici says, "You will accomplish more by kind words and a courteous manner than by anger or sharp rebuke, which should never be used except in necessity."

- St. Francis of Assisi tells us, "We have been called to heal wounds, to unite what has fallen apart, and to bring home those who have lost their way. Many who may seem to us to be children of the Devil will still become Christ's disciples."

- St. Teresa of Avila, who suffered her own persecution and rejection from the very ranks of those who were her followers, says, "Be proud that you are helping God to bear the cross and don't grasp at comforts. It is only mercenaries who expect to be paid by the day. Serve Him without pay."

- "Maintain good conduct among the Gentiles, so that if they speak of you as evildoers, they may observe your good works and glorify God on the day of visitation" (1 Pt 2:12).

By six weeks (forty-two days) from conception, the brain waves can be detected by an encephalogram, and the brain is controlling forty sets of muscles as well as the organs. The jaw forms, including teeth and taste buds. The unborn baby begins to swallow amniotic fluid. Fingers and toes are developing.

Let Us Pray

Heavenly Father, we lift up in prayer those who may have been wounded or scarred by the evil of abortion. Please change their hearts and heal their lives as only you can. Guide us in our pro-life effort to offer assistance and alternatives to those in need. Give us the gentleness and fortitude to offer kindness, especially when faced with anger or hostility. Help us to see others—especially our opponents—with *your* eyes. Amen.

Rejoice in Hope, Be Patient under Trial

Do not grow slack but be fervent in spirit; he whom you serve is the Lord. Rejoice in hope, be patient under trial, persevere in prayer.

—Romans 12:11–12 (NAB)

Reflection

- St. Thérèse of Lisieux says, "Trying to do good to people without God's help is no easier than making the sun shine at midnight. You discover that you've got to abandon all your own preferences, your own bright ideas, and guide souls along the road our Lord has marked out for them. You mustn't coerce them into some path of your own choosing."

- St. Augustine of Hippo quips, "If you should ask me what are the ways of God, I would tell you that the first is humility, the second is humility, and the third is still humility. Not that there are no other precepts to give, but if humility does not precede all that we do, our efforts are fruitless."

- St. Elizabeth Ann Seton tells us, "The gate of heaven is very low; only the humble can enter it."

- St. Paul urges us to behave as children of God and temples of the Holy Spirit, because that is what we are: "Do not conform yourselves to this age but be transformed by the renewal of your mind, that you may discern what is the will of God, what is good and pleasing and perfect" (Rom 12:2).

By six and one-half weeks (forty-five days) from conception, the unborn baby is making body movements, a full twelve weeks before the mother may notice such stirrings. By seven weeks, the chest and abdomen are fully formed. Swimming with a natural swimmer's stroke in the amniotic fluid, the baby now looks like a miniature human infant.

Let Us Pray

Dear Jesus, we pray that you keep close to your Sacred Heart all those who seek to defend innocent human life. Let us always rejoice in the hope of victory. In our disappointments, grant us patience and charity toward all. As St. Paul reminds us to "pray always," let us do so in the promise of your triumphant victory over death. Amen.

DAY ELEVEN

You Did It for Me

Amen, I say to you, whatever you did for one of
these least brothers of mine, you did for me.

—Matthew 25:40

Reflection

- St. Edith Stein (Sister Teresa Benedicta of the Cross)
  offered her prayer and her life as a proxy for the salvation of others—including the very Nazis who put her
  to death. She believed that the more a person is filled
  with divine love, the more she or he is uplifted to act on
  behalf of another, "for prayer is grounded in love." She
  writes, "For the Christian there is no stranger. Whoever
  is near us and needing us must be our neighbor; it does
  not matter whether he is related to us or not, whether
  we like him or not, whether he is morally worthy of our
  help or not. The love of Christ knows no limits. It never
  ends; it does not shrink from ugliness and filth. He came
  for sinners, not for the just. And if the love of Christ is
  in us we shall do as He did and seek the lost sheep."

- Pope St. Pius X tells us, "My last desire children, is that the love of our Lord dwell in you so that it will change you into so many apostles, zealous for His glory. You will be the treasure of your families, whom you will make happy by your good conduct."

- "For God so loved the world that he gave his only Son, so that everyone who believes in him might not perish but might have eternal life" (Jn 3:16).

From forty-four to forty-five days from conception, the buds of milk teeth appear, and the unborn baby's facial muscles develop. Eyelids begin to form, protecting the developing eyes. Elbows take shape. Internal organs are present but immature. Ninety-nine percent of muscles are present, each with its own nerve supply.

Let Us Pray

Heavenly Father, as members of the Mystical Body of Christ, we know that each and every human being—born and unborn—is made in your own image and likeness. Help us as people of life to treat everyone we meet with respect and kindness. Help us to spread the message of life, to offer our prayers and our deeds as a proxy for the good of others, and to do as St. Francis of Assisi exhorts, "Preach the Gospel at all times and when necessary, use words." Amen.

DAY TWELVE

Do Not Be Afraid

Now who is going to harm you if you are enthusiastic for what is good? But even if you should suffer because of righteousness, blessed are you. Do not be afraid or terrified with fear of them.

—1 Peter 3:13–14

Reflection

- Implore the help of Jesus Christ in all matters. St. Bernard of Clairvaux explains, "Nothing restrains anger, curbs pride, heals the wound of malice, bridles self-indulgence, quenches the passions, checks avarice and puts unclean thoughts to flight as does the name of Jesus." In other words, do everything in the name of Jesus, staying close to him and receiving the nourishment and grace needed through the holy sacraments of the Eucharist and Reconciliation. St. Francis de Sales tells us, "We shall steer safely through every storm, as long as our heart is right, our intention fervent, our courage steadfast, and our trust fixed in God."

- Blessed John Henry Cardinal Newman regarded even suffering and sickness as an opportunity to serve God: "Whatever, wherever I am, I can never be thrown away. If I am in sickness, my sickness may serve Him; if I am in sorrow, my sorrow may serve Him. . . . He does nothing in vain; He may prolong my life, He may shorten it; He knows what He is about. He may take away my friends, He may throw me among strangers, He may make me feel desolate, make my spirits sink, hide the future from me—still He knows what He is about."

- Blessed Mother Teresa of Calcutta reminds us that "prayer is the breath of life to our souls; holiness is impossible without it!"

- "The eyes of the Lord are in every place, keeping watch on the evil and the good" (Prv 15:3).

At around fifty-two days from conception, spontaneous movement begins. The unborn baby develops a whole collection of moves over the next four weeks including hiccupping, frowning, squinting, furrowing the brow, pursing the lips, moving individual arms and legs, turning the head, touching the face, breathing (without air), stretching, opening the mouth, yawning, and sucking.

Let Us Pray

Thank you, Lord, for giving us the opportunity to be your holy instrument of goodness and truth, and for the realization that even our shortcomings, our sickness, and the smallest and most insignificant acts can become a prayer of love for you and for those whom we are privileged to meet and serve this day. Grant us the perseverance and strength to do your will. In Jesus Christ, we pray. Amen.

Children Are a Gift— Parents Are Co-creators

Certainly sons are a gift from the Lord, the fruit of
the womb, a reward.

Like arrows in the hand of a warrior are the sons
born in one's youth.

Blessed is the man who has filled his quiver with
them.

He will never be shamed for he will destroy his
foes at the gate.

—Psalm 127:3–5

Reflection

- St. Francis de Sales asks, "When did God's love for you begin? When he began to be God. When did he begin to be God? Never, for He has always been without beginning and without end, and so He has always loved you from eternity."

- Blessed Pope John Paul II, in his encyclical *The Gospel of Life*, eloquently reminds married couples that they were nothing less than co-creators with God: "In affirming that the spouses, as parents, cooperate with God the Creator in conceiving and giving birth to a new human being, we are not speaking merely with reference to the laws of biology. Instead, we wish to emphasize that God himself is present in human fatherhood and motherhood quite differently than he is present in all other instances of begetting 'on earth.' . . . Thus a man and woman joined in matrimony become partners in a *divine undertaking*; through the act of procreation, God's gift is accepted and a new life opens to the future" (*The Gospel of Life*, 43; italics added).

- "God created mankind in his image; in the image of God he created them; male and female he created them" (Gn 1:27).

At eight weeks from conception, the child is a small-scale baby. He or she measures approximately three centimeters (one and one-eighth inches) and weighs one gram (one-thirtieth of an ounce), yet the baby is well-proportioned. Every organ is present. The baby's heartbeat is sturdy. The stomach produces digestive juices. The liver makes blood cells. The kidneys begin to function. The taste buds are forming.

Let Us Pray

Father in heaven, help us to see each and every human being as a unique and unrepeatable gift. May we always be people of joy who celebrate *all* life—even the surprises, and may we encourage married couples in our midst who, sometimes at great sacrifice, are welcoming new little ones into their homes and hearts.

Help us too, Father, to see *everyone*—most especially the challenging individuals in our lives—as the gift you designed them to be. Grant this through our Lord Jesus Christ, your Son who lives and reigns with you and the Holy Spirit, one God, now and forever. Amen.

Temples of
the Holy Spirit

Do you not know that your body is a temple of the holy Spirit within you, whom you have from God, and that you are not your own? For you have been purchased and at a price. Therefore glorify God in your body.

—1 Corinthians 6:19–20

Reflection

- St. Basil the Great writes of the Holy Spirit and his power in our lives: "To each who receive the Spirit, it is as if he alone received Him; yet the grace the Spirit pours out is quite sufficient for the whole of mankind." How's that for super power? In other words, we have no excuse to slough off or leave our duty to someone else—including those we may think are more able, skilled, or talented!

- St. John Vianney puts it more simply, "The Holy Spirit rests in the soul of the righteous just like the dove in her nest. He hatches good desires in a pure soul, as the dove hatches her young."

- "I will pour out water upon the thirsty ground, streams upon the dry land; I will pour out my spirit upon your offspring, and my blessing upon your descendants" (Is 44:3).

At eight and one-half weeks from conception, the unborn baby's fingerprints are being engraved. The eyelids and palms of hands are sensitive to touch.

Let Us Pray

Thank you, Father, for the gift of your Holy Spirit. How often we forget in our day-to-day living that we are members of your Mystical Body and have the power to bring Christ to the world and the world to Christ. Sometimes we may feel tongue-tied when it comes to witnessing our faith and beliefs to others. But you promised to be with us *always,* and so we pray that you will send your Holy Spirit to guide us in all that we do in Jesus' name. Help us always to remember that every person is sacred because each is made in your own image and likeness. Amen.

The Beatitudes

All your works give you thanks, LORD, and your
faithful bless you.

—Psalm 145:10

Reflection

*   "When he saw the crowds, he went up on the moun-
    tain and after he had sat down, his disciples came to
    him. He began to teach them, saying:

    'Blessed are the poor in spirit,
    >   for theirs is the kingdom of heaven
    Blessed are they who mourn,
    >   for they will be comforted.
    Blessed are the meek,
    >   for they will inherit the land.
    Blessed are they who hunger and thirst for
        righteousness,
    >   for they will be satisfied.
    Blessed are the merciful,
    >   for they will be shown mercy.

Blessed are the clean of heart,
    for they will see God.
Blessed are the peacemakers,
    for they will be called children of God.
Blessed are they who are persecuted for the sake
    of righteousness,
    for theirs is the kingdom of heaven.
Blessed are you when they insult you and persecute you and utter every kind of evil against you
[falsely] because of me. Rejoice and be glad, for
your reward will be great in heaven. Thus they
persecuted the prophets who were before you'"
(Mt 5:1–12).

- Is there someone in my family, circle of friends, neigh-
borhood, or community, who needs my listening ear,
helping hands, or caring heart? Just for today, beginning right this minute, offer these twenty-four hours
to God, as a small sacrifice for those who may be persecuted or abandoned.

- St. Teresa of Avila teaches, "Let nothing disturb you,
nothing frighten you; all things are passing; God never
changes."

By eight to eight and one-half weeks from conception,
of the four thousand five hundred structures in the adult
body, four thousand are now present in the unborn baby.

The skeleton of the arms, legs, and spine begins to stiffen as bone cells are added.

Let Us Pray

Lord Jesus, where do I begin? I feel so helpless and weak. I want to do good, but without your grace, I am powerless. Please show me the way and help me to offer everything I do today—even the chores and tasks I don't want to do—as a gift for you.

Help me to see that even sweeping the floor, changing a diaper, being stalled in traffic, or showing concern and kindness for someone difficult to love can be a great gift of grace if offered to you. Amen.

DAY SIXTEEN

Seeking Our
Mother's Help

Hail Mary, full of Grace, the Lord is with you.
Blessed are you among women and blessed is the
fruit of your womb.

—Hail Mary (see Lk 1:28)

Reflection

- St. Thomas Aquinas, a Doctor of the Church and
  one of the greatest theologians of all time, declares
  of Mary, "As sailors are guided by a star to the port,
  so Christians are guided to heaven by Mary. . . . The
  Blessed Virgin, by becoming the Mother of God,
  received a kind of infinite dignity because God is
  infinite; this dignity therefore is such a reality that a
  better one is not possible, just as nothing can be better
  than God."

- Blessed Pope John Paul II had a personal and special
  devotion to the Blessed Virgin Mary. In his "Letter to

the Carmelites" during the Marian year, he writes, "Assumed into Heaven, she now extends the protective mantle of her mercy over her children who are still on pilgrimage toward the holy mountain of glory."

- St. Jerome reminds us, "Mary not only comes to us when called but even spontaneously advances to meet us."

- "Elizabeth, filled with the Holy Spirit, cried out in a loud voice and said, 'Most blessed are you among women and blessed is the fruit of your womb'" (Lk 1:41–42).

At nine weeks from conception, medical evidence reveals that the unborn baby will bend fingers around an object placed in his/her palm. Unique fingerprints appear. Thumb-sucking may occur.

Let Us Pray

Blessed Mother, Christ gave us to you from the Cross on Calvary to watch over and pray for us. Please pray for our nation that has legalized the killing of more than one million little ones each year. Pray for America, our president, judges, and elected leaders, that by God's grace they will be converted to do all in their power to restore the right to life of every baby in the womb.

Pray, too, for us that we will be enlightened by the Holy Spirit with the grace and strength to vote and participate as citizens in whatever way we are able; choose elected leaders who will advocate for the rights of *all* human beings, born and unborn; and protect the family. Amen.

The Breath of Life

Just as you do not know how the life breath enters the human frame in the mother's womb, so you do not know the work of God, who is working in everything.

—Ecclesiastes 11:5

Reflection

- In today's culture, we confront many so-called experts who claim that human existence is mere chance or biological happenstance. Pope Benedict XVI eloquently reminds us, "We are not some casual meaningless product of evolution. Each of us is the result of a thought of God. Each of us is willed, each of us is loved, each of us is necessary."

- St. Augustine exhorts, "Creation is a great book. Look above you; look below you! Note it; read it! God . . . didn't write that book with ink. Instead, he set before your eyes the things that he had made. Can you ask for a louder voice than that? Why, heaven and earth cry out to you, 'God made me!'"

• "Notice how the flowers grow. They do not toil or spin. But I tell you, not even Solomon in all his splendor was dressed like one of them. If God so clothes the grass in the field that grows today and is thrown into the oven tomorrow, will he not much more provide for you, O you of little faith?" (Lk 12:27–28).

At ten weeks from conception, the unborn baby's body is sensitive to touch. He/she squints, swallows, puckers up the brow, and frowns. Eyelids, fingerprints, and even fingernails are evident.

Let Us Pray

Dear Father in heaven, it is awesome to contemplate the mystery of your creation. From the placement of the planet; to the sun, the moon and the stars; to the intricate detail of the smallest insect and the largest mammal, *everything* of your making was designed with precision and purpose. Your creation of a human being is a sacred masterpiece—each person infused with a soul and the breath of life—unique and unrepeatable!

Thank you for the gift of *my* life. Thank you for all those who loved and cared for me—my parents, grandparents, extended family, and friends. Thank you for the teachers and mentors who helped instill the *gift* of faith and a sense of awe at the beauty of your creation. Most especially, thank you for all of those who helped me to know *you*. Amen.

The Fifth Commandment— Pray for God's Mercy

You shall not kill.

—Exodus 20:13

Reflection

- God is clear about the taking of human life. He is so clear that he gave us not a suggestion but a commandment. In addition, scripture throughout the Old and New Testament reminds us that "anyone who sheds the blood of a human being, by a human being shall that one's blood be shed; For in the image of God have human beings been made" (Gn 9:6).

- The act of abortion is a grievous sin. We pray for those who perform and participate in abortion, as well as those who may have influenced, encouraged, or coerced a pregnant mother to abort her child. We pray too, for those who may have been so indifferent, silent, or uncaring that abortion was seen as the only solution.

- As Christians, we are called upon to care for our brothers and sisters who may be less fortunate or in need: "Cursed be anyone who deprives the resident alien, the orphan or the widow of justice!" (Dt 27:19). Let us never be indifferent or nonchalant about the gift of new life and let us offer kindness and compassion in whatever way possible.

- And when we fail in our efforts or cause insult, hurt, or harm to another, we ask for God's forgiveness and mercy. Blessed Pope John XXIII was called the "Good Pope" and was revered and loved by people of all faiths for his warmth and compassion. In speaking of the unlimited mercy of God he says, "In Psalm 136 this mercy, this 'steadfast love,' is referred to no fewer than twenty-six times, for his mercy endures forever. And this is what strengthens us in the endeavor to preserve interior peace."

By eleven weeks from conception, the unborn baby now practices breathing, since he or she will have to breathe air immediately after birth. The baby urinates, and stomach muscles can now contract. Vocal chords and taste buds form. Facial expressions and even smiles are evident.

Let Us Pray

Lord, forgive me for the times I have been angry or my actions were hurtful to others. Forgive my indifference that has caused hurt and pain. Please give me the grace to treat everyone I meet this day with *your* love and kindness. Keep my guardian angel close by to prevent me from wrongdoing when my patience grows thin or I feel mistreated or rejected and want to lash back. Amen.

DAY NINETEEN

Do Good to All

Let us not grow tired of doing good, for in due time we shall reap our harvest, if we do not give up. So then, while we have the opportunity, let us do good to all.

—Galatians 6:9–10

Reflection

- Remember the words of Blessed Mother Teresa of Calcutta: "Do something beautiful for God."

- St. Padre Pio of Pietrelcina also speaks to us: "Do everything for the love of God and His glory without looking at the outcome of the undertaking. Work is judged not by its result, but by its intention."

- Reflect on these words of Blessed Mother Teresa: "To those who say they admire my courage, I have to tell them that I would not have any if I were not convinced that each time I touch the body of a leper, a body that reeks with a foul stench, I touch Christ's body, the same Christ I receive in the Eucharist."

- "I am convinced that neither death, nor life, not angels, nor principalities, nor present things, nor future things, nor powers, nor height, nor depth, nor any other creature will be able to separate us from the love of God in Christ Jesus, our Lord" (Rom 8:35–39).

At twelve weeks from conception, though too small to be felt by the mother, the baby reaches the peak frequency of movement. The baby's sex can be visually determined, and the child's eyes, ears, and face begin to display distinctive characteristics. He or she can kick, turn the feet, curl and fan the toes, make a fist, move the thumbs, bend the wrists, turn the head, open the mouth, and press the lips tightly together.

Let Us Pray

As I go about my daily chores and challenges, help me today, Lord, to do everything out of love for you. Please use even my shortcomings and downfalls to work for good, as only you can. And when things become too difficult or uncomfortable, or I'm tempted to reach for an excuse, help me to offer my discouragement, frustration, and fatigue for your honor and glory. Help me to remember that even if I don't accomplish anything noble or noticeable, the smallest act becomes sacred in your eyes if I but offer it to you. Amen.

Love for God's Little Ones

Whoever causes one of these little ones who believe in me to sin, it would be better for him to have a great millstone hung around his neck and to be drowned in the depths of the sea. Woe to the world because of things that cause sin! Such things must come, but woe to the one through whom they come!

—Matthew 18:6–7

Reflection

- Mother Angelica, the down-to-earth, tell-it-like-it-is founder of Eternal Word Television Network (EWTN), has this to say about seeing Jesus and seeking goodness even in the unlovable situations: "The greatest evils today are fear and lukewarmness. Jesus said, 'I wish you were hot or cold, but you are lukewarm and I will vomit you from my mouth' (Rev 3:15–16). We have a fantastic amount of lukewarmness in the world today, because we don't see Jesus in the Present Moment. Every moment you are meeting Jesus face to face. Some woman told me the other day, 'Are you telling me that mean kid of mine is Jesus?' Yes, hidden in that kid is Jesus. It is your duty to bring Him out with love, patience, and compassion."

- St. Vincent de Paul recounts his own efforts at self-discipline: "I turned to God and earnestly begged him to convert this irritable and forbidding trait of mine. I also asked for a kind and amiable spirit. And with the grace of our Lord, by giving a little attention to checking the hot-blooded impulses of my personality, I have been at least partly cured of my gloomy disposition."

- "Children's children are the crown of the elderly, and the glory of children is their parentage" (Prv 17:6).

By twelve weeks from conception, the unborn baby is about three inches long, weighing approximately two ounces. Fine hair begins to grow on the upper lip, chin, and eyebrows. The baby swallows and responds to skin stimulations.

Let Us Pray

Heavenly Father, help us to teach our children, grandchildren, godchildren, and those who may look to us for guidance to have reverence and respect for every human being, born and unborn, from the youngest to the oldest. Help us never to cause scandal or confusion by acquiescing in the notion that some human beings may be *unwanted* or *better off dead*. And help us most especially when those who appear unreasonable or unlovable challenge us. Help us to always respond as witnesses of love. Amen.

God's Promise

If then my people, upon whom my name has been pronounced, humble themselves and pray, and seek my face and turn from their evil ways, I will hear them from heaven and pardon their sins and heal their land.

—2 Chronicles 7:14

Reflection

- St. Paul of the Cross encourages us, "Entrust yourself entirely to God. He is a Father and most loving Father at that, who would rather let heaven and earth collapse than abandon anyone who trusted in Him."

- The scourge of legal abortion has forever scarred our once-beautiful nation. More than one million babies have been legally killed each year since the January 22, 1973, Supreme Court decision which struck down all laws protecting mothers and babies from abortionists and gave us the most liberal law in the world (legal through all nine months).[†] Each year more evil methods are promoted to end lives. Young mothers are pressured to take chemicals or use various devices that cause untold numbers of silent abortions. Sadder still is the government-sponsored shipments of contraceptives and abortifacients being routinely sent to the Third World, whose people are seeking basic necessities and assistance.

- "Blessed is the man who perseveres in temptation, for when he has been proved he will receive the crown of life that he promised to those who love him" (Jas 1:12).

At thirteen weeks from conception, the unborn baby's face has filled out and facial expressions may resemble the parents'. The baby is active but still too small for the mother to feel movement.

Let Us Pray

Lord, please heal our nation as only you can. Help us begin within our own families and communities to broadcast

[†]   After "viability" of the unborn child, an individual state can, if it chooses to do so, enact laws to protect the unborn child but abortion must be allowed if the life or "health" of the mother is at stake. The Supreme Court defined "health" as "the medical judgment that may be exercised in light of all factors—physical, emotional psychological, familial, and the woman's age—relevant to the well-being of the patient. All these factors may relate to health" (Doe v. Bolton, 410 US 179 [1973]).

the truth all across America and beyond. Help us to live as people of hope and faith in this culture of death that surrounds us.

And please, Lord, help us restore this great nation as a beacon of freedom to others around the world. Help us renew the eloquent words of the Declaration of Independence, which declares that all human beings are *created by God* and possessed with an inalienable right . . . to life. Amen.

Defend the Lowly and Fatherless

Defend the lowly and the fatherless;
render justice to the afflicted and needy.
Rescue the lowly and the poor;
deliver them from the hand of the wicked.

—Psalm 82:3–4

Reflection

- "If you remain indifferent in time of adversity, your strength will depart from you. Rescue those who are being dragged to death, and from those tottering to execution, withdraw not" (Prv 24:10–11, NAB).

- St. Philip Neri reminds us, "Cast yourself into the arms of God and be very sure that if he wants anything of you, he will fit you for the work and give you strength."

- St. Francis de Sales says, "Nothing is so strong as gentleness, nothing so gentle as real strength."

- Write to one of your elected officials, urging him or her to work for laws that will protect the unborn and other most vulnerable members of our human family. Be as specific as you can about a current issue under discussion.

At fourteen weeks from conception, the heart pumps several quarts of blood through the baby's body every day. The unborn baby's eyebrows have formed, and eye movement can be detected.

Let Us Pray

Father in heaven, show us the way. Send your Holy Spirit to guide us. Help us not to become overwhelmed or paralyzed but to see that even the most insignificant of acts, if offered to you, can be a prayer for those in need. Help us, Lord, and give us your wisdom that we may speak and work with confidence and boldness, but always with a gentle kindness. Amen.

Adopt an Unborn Baby

Let the children come to me; do not prevent them,
for the kingdom of God belongs to such as these.

—Mark 10:14

Reflection

- Venerable Archbishop Fulton J. Sheen spent his last years speaking out against the evil of abortion and urged Christians to adopt the life of an unborn baby by reciting this prayer daily: "Jesus, Mary and Joseph, I love you very much. I beg you to spare the life of the preborn child that I have spiritually adopted who is in danger of abortion."

- Blessed Mother Teresa of Calcutta teaches, "Prayer does not demand that we interrupt our work, but that we continue working as if it were a prayer. Make everything a prayer!"

- "Keep me safe, O God; in you I take refuge" (Ps 16:1).

At fifteen weeks from conception, a wild production of nerve cells begins and continues for a month. A second surge will occur at twenty-five weeks. By now the baby has an adult's taste buds.

Let Us Pray

Dear Lord, please allow me to spiritually adopt a little one (*fetus* in Latin) who is threatened by legal abortion today. Use my prayer today for the safety and protection of this baby and surround the mother in distress with your angels of mercy and love.

Help me never to be indifferent or hardened by legal abortion. Help me never to appear self-righteous or haughty to those who are not pro-life. They are your children, too. Help me to pray for them and to see them in *your* eyes, as misinformed brothers and sisters in need of kindness and love. Amen.

Angels to Protect

See, I am sending an angel before you, to guard you on the way and bring you to the place I have prepared. Be attentive to him and obey him.

—Exodus 23:20–21

Reflection

- St. Jerome writes, "So valuable to heaven is the dignity of the human soul that every member of the human race has a guardian angel from the moment the person begins to be."

- St. Basil the Great adds, "An angel is put in charge of every believer, provided we do not drive him out by sin. He guards the soul like an army."

- "No evil shall befall you,
  no affliction come near your tent.
  For God commands the angels
  to guard you in all your ways.
  With their hands they shall support you,

lest you strike your foot against a stone" (Ps 91:10–12, NAB).

At sixteen weeks, or four months from conception, the unborn baby is now only five and one-half inches long, weighing approximately five ounces. He or she is actively moving about inside the safety of the womb. The baby turns, kicks, and even somersaults—some of which can now be felt by the mother.

Let Us Pray

Heavenly Father, we sometimes feel overwhelmed by the sheer audacity of the evil that confronts us daily in the surrounding culture of death. Yet scripture tells us to trust in you and to rely on the guardian angel that you provide to protect us. Lord, bless our efforts as we strive to offer hope and help to those in need in this movement for life. We pray:

> Angel of God my Guardian Dear
> to whom God's love commits me here.
> Ever this day be at my side,
> to light and to guard, to rule and to guide. Amen.

Behold, the Virgin Shall Bear a Child

You have found favor with God. Behold, you will conceive in your womb and bear a son, and you shall name him Jesus. He will be great and will be called Son of the Most High.

—Luke 1:30–32

Reflection

- The lessons of the birth of Jesus in a stable are many: from Mary's humble *fiat*, "May it be done unto me according to your word" (Lk 1:38), to Joseph's trust in the message of the angel, to the lowly stable with only a food trough and hay to hold the newborn king. What a place for a king and the mother of God!

- In reference to Mary, Blessed John Henry Cardinal Newman writes, "No one has access to the Almighty as his mother has; none has merit such as hers. Her son will deny her nothing that she asks; and herein lies her power. While she defends the Church, neither height nor depth, neither men nor evil spirits, neither great monarchs, nor craft of man, nor popular violence, can avail to harm us; for human life is short, but Mary reigns above, a Queen forever."

- In his book *The World's First Love: Mary, Mother of God*, Venerable Archbishop Fulton J. Sheen writes, "[Mary] is the earthly principle of love that leads to the heavenly principle of love. The relation between her and God is something like the relation between rain and the earth. Rain falls from the heavens, but the earth produces. Divinity comes from heaven; the human nature of the Son of God comes from her. We speak of 'mother earth' since it gives life through heaven's gift of the sun; then why not also recognize the Madonna of the World, since she gives us the Eternal Life of God?"

By sixteen weeks or four months from conception, the bone marrow is now beginning to form and the unborn baby's heart is pumping twenty-five quarts of blood a day.

Let Us Pray

Father in heaven, help me to see Jesus in my own surroundings. Help me to bring him into the world I live in and to be Mary-like as I strive to be a witness of faith and love. Help me to learn to submit *my* will and to trust, as Mary did, in God's will.

Blessed Mother, you are our mother, too. Please pray today for the mothers who do not know you. Pray for those who feel abandoned, abused, and alone. Pray for those who see abortion as a solution to a fearful pregnancy. Pray, too, for us in the pro-life movement, that we may be a witness of joy and love to all we meet today. Amen.

Joseph, Patron of Fathers and the Family

The angel of the Lord appeared to Joseph in a dream and said, "Rise, take the child and his mother, flee to Egypt, and stay there until I tell you. Herod is going to search for the child to destroy him." Joseph rose and took the child and his mother by night and departed for Egypt.

—Matthew 2:13–14

Reflection

- There are four separate instances, according to scripture, when an angel appeared to Joseph, the foster father of Jesus (Mt 1:20–24; 2:13–15; 2:19–21; 2:22). On each occasion, Joseph responded immediately, obeying the angel and acting quickly to protect the well-being and safety of Mary and the child, Jesus.

- Abandonment, abuse, and abortion are intrinsic evils. These evils demand intense spiritual warfare (Eph

6:12–18). We can't fight this battle alone. We should be calling on our friends in high places—the saints in heaven—to help and pray for us. And what better advocate could we turn to in prayer than the foster father of Jesus who is declared by the Church to be the patron of fathers and protector of families! For those children who do not have the presence of a supportive father in their lives, we can look to St. Joseph in prayer, and ask him to be that missing spouse and father figure to help instill faith and the love of God.

- "The angel of the Lord appeared in a dream to Joseph in Egypt and said, 'Rise, take the child and his mother and go to the land of Israel, for those who sought the child's life are dead.' He rose, took the child and his mother, and went to the land of Israel" (Mt 2:19–21).

By seventeen to eighteen weeks or four and one-half months from conception, the baby is still very small (less than eight inches in length), but can have dream (REM) sleep. Nostrils and toenails become visible.

Let Us Pray

Dear St. Joseph, please pray for us and for the well-being of our children and families. Ask the angels to watch over and guard us and help us to flee from all temptation and sin that could harm or separate us from the love of God. Amen.

DAY TWENTY-SEVEN

Pray for the Childless

And behold, Elizabeth, your relative, has also conceived a son in her old age, and this is the sixth month for her who was called barren; for nothing will be impossible for God.

—Luke 1:36–37

Reflection

- St. Edith Stein, a Carmelite nun of Jewish descent who was among the many gassed at Auschwitz, wisely observes, "In three different ways, a woman can fulfill the mission of motherliness: in marriage, in the practice of a profession that values human development . . . and under the veil as a spouse of Christ."

- What a divided world we live in today! On one hand, more than one million unborn babies each year are intentionally cut from their mother's womb and die by legal abortion because they are considered to be *unwanted*. On the other hand, more than two million couples in America are waiting to adopt a child, and that includes children of all races and those with special needs.

- There may be times of discouragement when we feel unable to pray. St. Thérèse, The Little Flower, suggests, "When I feel nothing, when I am incapable of praying or practicing virtue, then is the moment to look for small occasions, nothings that give Jesus more pleasure than the empire of the world, more even than martyrdom generously suffered. For example, a smile, a friendly word, when I would much prefer to say nothing at all or look bored."

- St. Thérèse encourages us to place our will in Jesus, writing, "It is He who you can embrace in everything that comes to you. I bless him, therefore, however my nature may protest. It will protest. There will be interior seething; there will be revolt of the senses; there will be moaning. But I shall bless him for everything, with all my will, united to his. I shall say in union with Mary, '*Fiat! Magnificat!*' in the midst of the tempest, and thus I shall always have a heavenly peace in the depths of my soul."

At seventeen to eighteen weeks (the end of the fourth month) the unborn baby's ears are functioning, and he or she hears the mother's heartbeat, as well as external sounds, such as music. The baby is also able to experience pain. Life-saving surgery has been successfully performed on babies at this age.

Let Us Pray

Heavenly Father, we remember in prayer today the heartache of those couples who would gladly welcome a new little one into their lives. Be with them and help them feel your presence and consoling love. Draw them to you and bless them for their faithfulness. Amen.

For Those Who Have Lost Children

The God of all grace who called you to his eternal glory through Christ [Jesus] will himself restore, confirm, strengthen and establish you after you have suffered a little. To him be dominion forever. Amen.

—1 Peter 5:10–11

Reflection

- St. Paul of the Cross tells us, "Those who suffer for the love of God help Jesus carry his cross and if they persevere they will share his glory in heaven."

- Blessed Mother Teresa of Calcutta reflects, "True love causes pain. Jesus, in order to give us the proof of his love, died on the cross. A mother, in order to give birth to her baby, has to suffer. If you really love one another, you will not be able to avoid making sacrifices."

- The prayer of St. Francis of Assisi calls us to be a healing presence for those who grieve the loss of a child:

> Lord, make me an instrument of your peace.
> Where there is hatred, let me sow love;
> Where there is injury, pardon;
> Where there is doubt, faith;
> Where there is despair, hope;
> Where there is darkness, light;
> Where there is sadness, joy.

Eighteen to twenty weeks or four and one-half to five
months from conception: The baby has grown in size to
approximately seven and one-half inches long and is fourteen ounces in weight. The mother can now feel her baby's
movements, including the baby's hiccups.

Let Us Pray

Heavenly Father, we lift up today those who have lost
children, born and unborn. Whether by miscarriage, sud-
den infant death, accident, or the tragedy of abortion, each
is a terrible loss. We pray for those children as well as
the parents, grandparents, family members, and friends
who mourn the death of a child. The pain of loss remains
always with them. Please wrap them in your tender arms
and heal their aching hearts; mend their wounds and help
them to offer their suffering to you. Amen.

Pray for the Family

People were bringing children to him that he might touch them, but the disciples rebuked them. When Jesus saw this he became indignant and said to them; "Let the children come to me; do not prevent them, for the kingdom of God belongs to such as these."

—Mark 10:13–14

Reflection

- Blessed Mother Teresa of Calcutta saw clearly the vital role of the family: "Peace and war begin at home. If we truly want peace in the world, let us begin by loving one another in our own families. If we want to spread joy, we need for every family to have joy." She also was not afraid to scold: "Everybody today seems to be in a hurry. No one has any time to give to others: children to their parents, parents to their children, spouses to each other. World peace begins to break down in the homes."

- In his book *Way to Happiness: An Inspiring Guide to Peace, Hope and Contentment*, Venerable Archbishop Fulton J. Sheen writes to parents, "God gives parents a child as so much plastic material that can be molded for good or evil. What if God placed a precious diamond in the hands of parents and told them to inscribe on it a sentence which would be read on the Last Day, and shown as an index of their thoughts and ideals. What caution they would exercise in their selection! And yet the example parents give their children will be that by which they will be judged on the Last Day. Parents hold the place of God in the house."

- Catholics know that marriage and parenting are a vocational call. When we respond in love to God's will, he will provide. Often parents and grandparents get caught up with lofty notions of goals and careers for their young, losing sight of the number one goal— not college, a great job, nor happiness here on earth— but heaven, where there is happiness and love for all eternity with God!

- Blessed Pope John Paul II was the first pope to write an encyclical letter to parents, to encourage them in their vocational call. He writes: "The family has a special role to play . . . from birth to death. It is truly the sanctuary of life; the place in which life—the gift of God—can be properly welcomed and protected against the many attacks to which it is exposed and can develop in accordance with what constitutes authentic human growth" (*Centesimus Annus*, 39).

At five months from conception, each side of the brain has a billion nerve cells. If a sound is especially loud, the unborn baby may jump in reaction to it. Thumb-sucking has been observed during the fifth month.

Let Us Pray

Heavenly Father, today we lift up our own families, the children in our lives, the parents, grandparents, godparents, and extended family. You know each one by name, and you know, too, the imminent challenges, temptations, and crosses they face. Please provide them with your grace so that they will endure and prevail as they strive for heaven. Amen.

For Those in the Pro-Life Movement

Let the word of Christ, rich as it is, dwell in you. In wisdom made perfect, instruct and admonish one another. Sing gratefully to God from your hearts in psalms, hymns, and inspired song. Whatever you do, whether in speech or in action, do it in the name of the Lord Jesus. Give thanks to God the Father through him.

—Colossians 3:15–16 (NAB)

Reflection

* St. Edith Stein says, "Millions of children today are homeless and orphaned, even though they do have a home and a mother. They hunger for love and eagerly await a guiding hand to draw them out of dirt and misery into purity and light. How could it be otherwise than that our great holy mother the Church should open her arms wide to take these beloved of the Lord to her heart? But for this she needs human

arms and human hearts, maternal arms and maternal hearts."

- Blessed Mother Teresa of Calcutta and the Missionaries of Charity were known to rescue babies who had survived late-term abortions. They went to abortion places at the end of the day and brought to their home for homeless children the infants who were found still breathing. She said of her street work when accepting the Nobel Peace Prize, "We are fighting abortion by adoption, we have saved thousands of lives. We have sent words to all the clinics, to the hospitals, police stations—please don't destroy the child, we will take the child. We will get a home for the child."

- "Consider it all joy, my brothers, when you encounter various trials, for you know that the testing of your faith produces perseverance. And let perseverance be perfect, so that you may be perfect and complete, lacking in nothing. Come to its perfection so that you may be fully mature and lacking in nothing" (Jas 1:2–4).

By five to six months from conception, the unborn baby practices breathing by inhaling amniotic fluid into its developing lungs. The baby will increase seven times in weight and nearly double in height.

Let Us Pray

Dear Lord, today we lift up in prayer the babies scheduled for abortion and their mothers who may feel pressured or coerced into aborting their little ones. May their guardian angels protect them from harm. We pray, too, for those suffering from previous involvement in abortion—be they the mother or father of a child, family member, counselor, or friend who advised abortion as a solution. In Jesus' name may those of us involved in the pro-life movement never fail to offer assistance and compassion to those in need. Amen.

DAY THIRTY-ONE

Pray for Adoption

So the woman took the child and nursed him. When the child grew, she brought him to Pharaoh's daughter, and he became her son. She named him Moses; for she said, "I drew him out of the water."

—Exodus 2:9–10

Reflection

- Blessed Mother Teresa of Calcutta's work with the poor is a great witness to the sacredness of human life and the goodness of adoption: "Unborn children are among the poorest of the poor. They are so close to God. I see God in the eyes of every child. Every unwanted child is welcomed by us. We then find homes for these children through adoption."

- Blessed Mother Teresa also says, "The first person in the world to welcome Jesus, to recognize him in the womb of his own mother, was a child: John the

Baptist. It is wonderful; God chooses an unborn child to announce the coming of his redeeming Son."

• "For those who are led by the Spirit of God are children of God. For you did not receive a spirit of slavery to fall back into fear, but you received a spirit of adoption, through which we cry, 'Abba, Father!'" (Rom 8:14–15).

By six months from conception, fine hair grows on the eyebrows and head. Eyelash fringe appears. The unborn baby's weight is about twenty-two ounces; its height is about nine inches. Babies born at this age have survived.

Let Us Pray

Heavenly Father, help us to always be witnesses of life and to promote the goodness of adoption as part of your loving plan. Lord, help those who face a troubled pregnancy to be open to the possibility of adoption, to see it as an option for them and as a blessing for their baby. In Jesus' name we pray. Amen.

For Doctors, Nurses, and Caregivers

Jesus entered the house of Peter and saw his mother -in-law lying in bed with a fever. He touched her hand, the fever left her, and she rose and waited on him.

—Matthew 8:14–15

Reflection

- Physicians, nurses, health aids, and home caregivers are often on the front lines in offering aid and assistance to the sick and infirm. In caring for the needs of others, St. Vincent de Paul advises, "Let us love God, my brothers, let us love God. But let it be with the strength of our arms and the sweat of our brow. We must pass, my sisters, from affective love to effective love. And that is a love which takes flesh in works of charity, service of the poor which is undertaken with joy, constancy and tender love."

- And when our life's work appears discouraging or overwhelming, Blessed Mother Teresa encourages, "We ourselves feel that what we are doing is just a drop in the ocean. But if that drop was not there, I think the ocean would be less by that missing drop. We don't have to think in numbers. We can only love one person at a time, serve one person at a time."

- Pope Benedict XVI reminds us, "The world . . . is willing to listen to teachers when they are also witnesses. This is a lesson that must never be forgotten in the work of spreading the Gospel: We ourselves must be the first to live what we proclaim; we have to be a reflection of God's love."

- "For the spirit of God made me, the breath of the Almighty keeps me alive" (Jb 33:4).

By seven months (twenty-five to twenty-eight weeks) from conception, the unborn baby can recognize the mother's voice. The baby is using four of the five senses (vision, hearing, taste, and touch), opens and closes the eyes, knows the difference between waking and sleeping, and can relate to the moods of the mother.

Let Us Pray

Lord, we pray today for those physicians, nurses, health-care workers and caregivers who offer themselves to the service of others. Send your angels to watch over and protect them and lift them up when the weight of their tasks may seem overwhelming. Help them to see and treat each individual with dignity, concern, and respect—as if they were caring for Jesus himself. Amen.

DAY THIRTY-THREE

For Judges, Public Officials, and Leaders

Stand fast, with the truth as the belt around your waist, justice as your breastplate, and zeal to propagate the gospel of peace as your footgear.

—Ephesians 6:14–15 NAB

Reflection

- In Blessed Pope John XXIII's Christmas message in 1959, "Peace to Men of Good Will," he writes, "Social peace is solidly based on the mutual and reciprocal respect for the personal dignity of man. The disturbances which unsettle the internal peace of nations trace their origins chiefly to this source: that man has been treated almost exclusively as a machine, a piece of merchandise, a worthless cog in some great machine or a mere productive unit. It is only when the dignity of the person comes to be taken as the standard of value for man and his activities that the means will exist to settle civil discord and the often profound divisions between."

- St. Bernard of Clairvaux exhorts, "You can fight with confidence when you are sure of victory. With Christ and for Christ, victory is certain." And St. Augustine reminds us, "The crown of victory is promised only to those who engage in the struggle."

- And when we can do nothing more—pray! As St. Francis of Assisi insists, "Sanctify yourself and you will sanctify society!" Pray!

- "Only with prayer—prayer that storms the heavens for justice and mercy, prayer that cleanses our hearts and souls, will the *culture of death* that surrounds us today, be replaced with the *culture of life*" (USCCB, "Pastoral Plan for Pro-life Activities"; italics added).

At eight months (thirty-two to thirty-six weeks) from conception, the unborn baby's skin becomes pink and smooth. The pupils of the eye respond to light.

Let Us Pray

Dear Lord, please send your Holy Spirit to guide those who are in positions of authority. We pray for all judges, and for those who hold public office or form public policy. Open their hearts to the truth and guide their decision-making, helping them to see the intrinsic dignity of every human being. Give them the strength and courage to work for the rights and lives of those who are most vulnerable—the weak and infirm, the elderly and dependent, the poor and homeless, and those who are not yet born.

Holy Spirit, we look to you for guidance. Help us to do all in our power as citizens of this great nation to be your hands and feet. Help us not to be ambivalent or apathetic in our God-given right to act as responsible citizens. Help us to know what we can do this very day to offer hope and help, justice and mercy to those in need. Amen.

For Pastors and Religious Leaders

Go, therefore, and make disciples of all nations, baptizing them in the name of the Father, and of the Son, and of the holy Spirit, teaching them to observe all that I have commanded you. And behold, I am with you always, until the end of the age.

—Matthew 28:19–20

Reflection

- More than ever in this culture of death our religious leaders, pastors, spiritual directors, and priests need our support and our prayers—daily, if possible. Think of who does not want them to be faithful to the Word of God and who constantly tempts them to sin. The devil does not prey on those who are already indifferent or apathetic to God's love, but on the ones who are eager to serve God. Let us pray that their guardian angels will surround and protect these ministers of faith.

- Servant of God Cardinal Francis Xavier Nguyen Van Thuan, who was imprisoned by the Vietnamese government for thirteen years and later expelled from his homeland, writes in his diary about serving with all his strength: "You have entrusted me with a mission, Lord, and you invite me to take responsibility by sharing in your redemptive work. Everything comes about through your infinite love. At the same time, everything also depends on my response. I must be conscious of the greatness of the mission entrusted to me, which is nothing less than Jesus' mission. 'As the Father has sent me, so I send you.'"

- St. Joseph of Cupertino reflects, "A preacher is like a trumpet that produces no tone unless one blows into it. Before preaching, pray to God, 'You are the Spirit and I am only the trumpet, and without your breath I can give no sound.'"

- "The disciples rejoiced when they saw the Lord. Jesus said to them again, 'Peace be with you. As the Father has sent me, so I send you.' And when he had said this, he breathed on them and said to them, 'Receive the Holy Spirit'" (Jn 20:20–22).

At eight months (twenty-nine to thirty-two weeks) from conception, the unborn baby's weight increases by one kilogram (more than two pounds) and his/her living quarters inside the mother's womb are becoming cramped.

Let Us Pray

Heavenly Father, please send your Holy Spirit to guide our priests and religious leaders. Give them the grace and spiritual courage to speak out—valiantly when necessary—in support of life and family. So many today, including good people of faith, are ignorant or misinformed about the truth and beauty of human life and the sacredness of marriage between a man and a woman. We need shepherds with conviction and courage who will lead. By their words and their witness, help them to be beacons of light and life in this darkened world. Help them to speak with clarity about the intrinsic evil of abortion and the hidden destructive power of artificial contraceptives. In Jesus' name we pray. Amen.

Prayer for Conversion

Have mercy on me, God, in accord with your merciful love;
in your abundant compassion blot out my transgressions.
Thoroughly wash away my guilt;
and from my sin cleanse me.

—Psalm 51:3–4

Reflection

- Christians are people of faith and hope. Thus, we must act and pray accordingly, rejecting the notion that there are those so hardened by sin that they are incapable of conversion. Let us never underestimate the effectiveness of prayer and the miraculous power of God! St. John Vianney tells us, "God is always almighty. He can at all times work miracles, and he would work them now as in the days of old were it not that faith is lacking."

- Cardinal Francis Xavier Nguyen Van Thuan of Vietnam, wrote in his diary, *Prayers of Hope: Words of Courage*: "A sign attracts attention; the more luminous, the more it stands out and the greater its impact. . . . A sign's power lies in its 'difference'; a distinct color, the brilliance of a light beam, a particular sound, etc. Without this, these signals would not attract attention. If I am no different in some way or am afraid to be, I will not be a recognizable sign. No one will pay attention to me. . . . The Lord asks me to be a sign showing the Father in Heaven to all people."

- Dr. Bernard Nathanson, Jewish by birth and atheist by choice, founded the National Abortion Rights Action League. As a practicing obstetrician/gynecologist, Dr. Nathanson directed the first and largest abortion facility in the United States in New York City. He later acknowledged, "I am responsible for over 60,000 deaths by abortion." In speaking of his conversion to a pro-life vision he recalled, "There is no doubt in my mind that it was the prayers of Christians—including those who quietly prayed outside my clinic—that caused my pro-life conversion." Here, indeed, is an example of the power of a silent sign. Dr. Nathanson was baptized and welcomed into the Catholic Church by Cardinal John O'Connor of New York. He spent the remainder of his life traveling and speaking for the pro-life cause, refusing any stipend or compensation.

- "Whoever brings back a sinner from the error of his way will save his soul from death and will cover a multitude of sins" (Jas 5:20).

By eight months (twenty-nine to thirty-two weeks) from conception, the unborn baby's fingernails reach to the tip of the finger. The skin begins to thicken, with a layer of fat stored underneath for insulation and nourishment.

Let Us Pray

Dear Lord, help us to be a prayerful presence to all of those we meet today. We pray especially for those who have no one to pray for them: the mother scheduled for abortion, her helpless baby, the abortionist, the medical staff, and those involved in this gruesome deadly act. We pray, too, for those who may advise and influence a fearful mother to have an abortion. Please forgive their wrongs and send your angels of truth and light that they may be converted to know you and realize the errors of their ways. Just as you touched Saul, who was then converted and became Paul; so, too, touch and change the hearts of those caught in the scourge of abortion. Amen.

For the Homebound, Shut-In, and Imprisoned

Three times I begged the Lord about this, that it might leave me, but he said to me, "My grace is sufficient for you, for power is made perfect in weakness." I will rather boast most gladly of my weaknesses, in order that the power of Christ may dwell with me.

—2 Corinthians 12:8–9

Reflection

- In his book *Crossing the Threshold of Hope*, Blessed Pope John Paul II tells us, "God is always on the side of suffering. His omnipotence is manifested precisely in the fact that He freely accepted suffering. He could have chosen not to do so. He could have chosen to demonstrate His omnipotence even at the moment of the Crucifixion. In fact, it was proposed to Him: 'Let the Messiah, the King of Israel, come down now from the cross that we may see and believe' (Mk 15:32). But he did not accept the challenge. . . . Yes, God is Love and precisely for this He gave His Son, to reveal Himself completely as Love."

- St. Thérèse of Lisieux (The Little Flower) was a Carmelite nun who lived a cloistered life until her early death from tuberculosis at age twenty-four. She was later declared one of the greatest saints of modern times, not for any mighty acts of heroism, but for living each day in her "little way," offering every chore and challenge, interruption and irritation, as a prayer. "It is a way of childlike self-surrender, the way of a child who sleeps, afraid of nothing, in its father's arms."

- Blessed Mother Teresa of Calcutta credits the success of her work to her silent partners—people who were sick, suffering, or in persistent pain, and who agreed to offer their confinement or hurt for one of the sisters of the Missionaries of Charity.

- Blessed Mother Teresa tells us that "wherever God has put you, that is your vocation. It is not what we do but how much love we put into it."

At eight months (twenty-nine to thirty-two weeks) from conception, the unborn baby swallows a gallon of amniotic fluid each day and often hiccups. Though movement is limited due to the cramped quarters, the baby's kicks are stronger, and the mother may be able to feel an elbow or heel against her abdomen.

Let Us Pray

Dear Lord, please help me to see that even when I am confined by illness, homebound, unable to perform my daily duties or enjoy outside activities, all this, if offered to you for your honor and glory, can be a great source of grace and a channel of miraculous power. Help me to see that the little, most insignificant deed is packed with power and healing when offered to you. Though I may never see the good results of my prayer or offering up here on earth, I entrust all to you. Amen.

For Those Who Have Died

If for this life only we have hoped in Christ, we are the most pitiable people of all.

—1 Corinthians 15:19 (NAB)

Reflection

- St. Thérèse of Lisieux tells us not only to pray for those who have died, but to ask them to pray for us: "I believe that the blessed in heaven have a great compassion for our wretchedness; they remember that when they were frail and mortal like us they committed the same faults, endured the same struggles, and their fraternal love becomes greater even than it was on earth which is why they do not cease to protect us and pray for us."

- St. Maximilian Kolbe reminds us, "We must sanctify ourselves at every moment, for we know not if the next will be ours. It is for us to become holy here and now, for we cannot be certain whether we will be here this evening. The better we fulfill our obligations, the more we give glory to God and respond to the will of the Immaculata [the Blessed Mother]. So important is the present moment that we must continually remind ourselves of it as the means of sanctification."

- When Blessed Pope John XXIII was a bishop and upon hearing the news of his father's death, he wrote to his mother and family: "Today, as soon as I received the sad telegram I had to go alone into my chapel and weep like a child. Now I am feeling a little calmer, but my tears are still ready to flow. . . . Our dear father has become invisible to our eyes, but he still lives with us. He loves us, protects us and awaits us in heaven."

- "For God so loved the world that he gave his only Son, so that everyone who believes in him might not perish but might have eternal life" (Jn 3:16).

Approaching the ninth month, the baby gains about one-half pound per week as she/he prepares for birth. The bones in the child's head are soft and flexible to more easily mold for the journey down the birth canal.

Let Us Pray

Heavenly Father, we lift up in prayer all of those who have died. We pray especially for our family members and loved ones. Please forgive any transgressions or wrongs they may have committed and welcome them into your merciful, loving arms.

We pray, too, for those forgotten souls who have no one to pray on their behalf (perhaps a former neighbor, teacher, mentor, or someone who may have been unkind or hurt us, or someone we may have hurt).

We pray too for the unborn babies who will die by abortion today. Have mercy on any mother who choses abortion in desperation, and welcome the little one into your loving arms. Amen.

For Pregnancy Counselors and Those on the Front Lines

You are standing firm in one spirit, with one mind struggling together for the faith of the gospel, not intimidated in any way by your opponents. This is proof to them of destruction, but of your salvation. And this is God's doing.

—Philippians 1:27–28

Reflection

- So often we may feel inadequate to counsel another, especially regarding something as intimate and profound as a pregnancy. But amazingly, our inadequacy is a good thing. God can use our incompetence to achieve his good far more than any misguided confidence we may have. St. Thérèse, the Little Flower, says, "Let us remain very remote from all that glitters. Let us love our littleness; let us love to feel nothing.

Then we shall be poor in spirit, and Jesus will come seeking us, however far away we are. He will transform us into flames of love!"

- In *Way to Happiness: An Inspiring Guide to Peace, Hope and Contentment*, Venerable Archbishop Fulton J. Sheen writes, "Many psychiatrists today know very well that all they have to do to help certain distressed minds is to listen to their stories. Convince the anxious heart that you know the secret of his anxiety and he is already half cured."

- And when we feel our counsel has been rebuffed, let us remember that we are part of God's movement, merely his instruments. St. Thérèse writes, "The intoxication of adulation turns a person's head, sometimes to the point of dizziness. When everything is successful, when a person receives nothing but applause, how could he not believe himself to be something or someone important? That is the danger of prominent positions. Therefore, bless the humiliation which disillusions and which saves."

- "But when he comes, the Spirit of truth, he will guide you to all truth" (Jn 16:13).

Approaching nine months, the unborn baby triggers labor, and birth occurs an average of 264 to 270 days after conception. Of the forty-five generations of cell divisions before adulthood, forty-one have already taken place. Only four more come before adolescence. Ninety percent of a person's development happens in the womb.

Let Us Pray

Dear Lord, help me to become one of your flames of love, especially when speaking to someone experiencing a troubled pregnancy. Help me to remember that my presence or guidance may be the *only* witness to encourage *life* to someone on the brink of an abortion decision. When occasions arise, when my witness may be needed, please send your Holy Spirit to give me the courage to speak or act in a way that will best stand for truth and your divine mercy. Amen.

God's Forgiveness and Mercy

If we acknowledge our sins, he is faithful and just and will forgive our sins and cleanse us from every wrongdoing.

—1 John 1:9

Reflection

- As Christians, we know firsthand about God's forgiveness and mercy. In our own lives and in confessing our own weaknesses and sins, we have felt the overpowering love of God. St. John Vianney says of mercy, "God's greatest pleasure is to pardon us." St. Thérèse of Lisieux tells us, "The good Lord is more eager to pardon a repentant sinner than a mother to rescue her child from the fire. In the sacrament of Penance, He gives us an infinite share of His mercy."

- The Holy Sacrifice of the Mass and the sacrament of the Eucharist are profound gifts from God. In the

Eucharist we are receiving Jesus himself into our hearts. The sacrament of Reconciliation (Penance) lifts the burden of our sinfulness and offers a grace that fortifies our resolve to withstand temptation and reject sin. Attending Mass and receiving the Eucharist as often as we can, along with confession (monthly if possible), are the best weapons we have to sustain and strengthen us in this life-and-death struggle.

- If we are to be God's Ambassadors (as St. Paul writes) in this great movement for life, we first must be fortified by prayer and the gift of the sacraments. In *Crossing the Threshold of Hope*, Blessed Pope John Paul II writes of God's mercy and the importance of prayer: "Through prayer God reveals Himself above all as mercy—that is, love that goes out to those who are suffering, love that sustains, uplifts, and invites us to trust."

- "Then I declared my sin to you; my guilt I did not hide. I said, 'I confess my transgressions to the Lord,' and you took away the guilt of my sin" (Ps 32:5).

Abortion fact: The United States Supreme Court ruling of January 22, 1973, (*Roe v. Wade* and *Doe v. Bolton*) struck down the laws in all fifty states, allowing abortion—for any reason—up to the moment of live birth. The father of the child, even if he is married to the mother, has no legal right to prevent the abortion.

Let Us Pray

Lord, help prepare us to worthily receive your sacraments and to encourage our children, grandchildren, and loved ones to do the same. We ask this through our Lord Jesus Christ, your Son, who lives and reigns with you in union with the Holy Spirit, one God forever and ever. Amen.

Bearers of Truth—
"Encourage One Another"

What eye has not seen, and ear has not heard and what has not entered the human heart what God has prepared for those who love him.

—1 Corinthians 2:9 (NAB)

Reflection

- Angelo Roncalli, who became Blessed Pope John XXIII, descended from Italian peasant origins and was known for his gentleness and kindness. He did not hesitate to speak out against evil, urging us always to be promoters of truth: "All the evils which poison men and nations and trouble so many hearts have a single cause and a single source: ignorance of the truth— and at times even more than ignorance a contempt for truth and a reckless rejection of it. . . . And yet, God gave each of us an intellect capable of attaining natural truth. If we adhere to this truth, we adhere to God himself, the author of truth, the lawgiver and ruler of our lives. But if we reject this truth, whether out of foolishness, neglect, or malice, we turn our backs on the highest good itself and on the very norm for right living."

- Blessed Mother Teresa of Calcutta tells us, "God pays attention to our love. Not one of us is indispensable. God has the means to do all things and to do away with the work of the most capable human being. We can work until we drop. We can work excessively. If what we do is not connected to love, however, our work is useless in God's eyes."

- Venerable Archbishop Fulton J. Sheen says, "Loving and serving are inseparable. Such service, too, is self-denying and ego-effacing. To continue helping day after day in the midst of reproach and opposition and rejection means that one is governed by a higher law than the desire of applause. Such service cannot be bought, for no gold could purchase it; neither does it need to be bought, for it is freely rendered."

- "What eye has not seen, and ear has not heard, and what has not entered the human heart, what God has prepared for those who love him" (1 Cor 2:9).

Abortion fact: Abortion is legal in America through all nine months of pregnancy. More than 1.3 million legal abortions occur in America each year. A sad irony is that more than two million couples are waiting to adopt a child, including children of all races and those with special needs.

Let Us Pray

Dear Father in heaven, thank you for the precious gift of faith and membership, through Christ, in your family. Help us never to be discouraged by the culture of death that surrounds us. Strengthen us that we may never tire in our efforts to build up your kingdom on earth. Send your angels to watch over and protect us in our efforts for life and family. Show us the way to restore our nation to its noble commitment to protecting all human beings, born and unborn. Help us to be witnesses to your truth and love, offering hope and life, encouragement and compassion to those who are poor in spirit. Grant all these graces through our Lord Jesus Christ, your Son, who lives and reigns with you and the Holy Spirit, one God, forever and ever. Amen.

Prayers for Life

Prayer of a Mom Who Lost a Child to Abortion

(Fr. Frank Pavone)

Lord God of Peace,
  I thank you for your love for me,
  Which is more tender than the love
  Of a mother for her child.
I thank you for your forgiveness,
  Which is more generous
  Than the forgiveness human beings can offer.
Thank you for helping me to know
  That I am not my abortion.
  Rather, I am your daughter, Beloved and Redeemed,
  For whom your Son would have died
  If I were the only one who needed salvation.
Save me always
  From the menacing voice of useless guilt and the
  oppressive force of shame.
Rather, lift me up in the light, peace, and grace
  Of the Risen Lord Jesus Christ,
  Who lives and reigns forever and ever. Amen.

Prayer of a Dad Who Lost a Child to Abortion

(Fr. Frank Pavone)

Lord God,
You are the Father of all,
And the source and pattern of all fatherhood.
You are our Provider, our Protector, our Encourager,
And you enable us to do the same for others.
I thank you for your mercy and healing,
Of which I stand in need
As I grieve my own lost fatherhood.
I turn to you, the Eternal Father,
And ask to be renewed
And to start again.
And I ask you to receive
Into your endless Life and Love, the child you once
    entrusted to me.
Give me new hope and new strength.
Always remind me
That you have more blessings for me in the future
Than there is pain in the past,
And that for everyone whom I may have failed to serve
    before,
You have many that you call me to serve
From today forward.

Lead me, Lord, in new hope and new strength.
I pray with confidence in Jesus' Name. Amen.

Spiritual Adoption of an Unborn Baby
(Venerable Archbishop Fulton J. Sheen)

Jesus, Mary and Joseph,
I love you very much
I beg you to save the life of the unborn baby
That I have spiritually adopted and is in *danger* of
  abortion.
Mary, Our Mother in Heaven
Pray for us,
and especially for your little ones
In danger of abortion. Amen.

Prayer to St. Gerard (patron of expectant mothers)

O good St. Gerard, powerful intercessor before the throne of God, wonder-worker of our day, I call upon you and seek your help. While on earth, you always fulfilled God's designs; help me, too, always to do God's holy will. Beseech the master of life, from whom all parenthood proceeds, to bless me with offspring, that I may raise up children to God in this life and heirs to the kingdom of God's glory in the life to come. Amen.

Prayer to Blessed Mother Teresa of Calcutta

Blessed Mother Teresa of Calcutta,
You allowed the thirsting love
Of Jesus on the Cross
To become a living flame
Within you and so became
The light of His love to all.
Obtain from the Heart of Jesus . . .
(make your request).
Teach me to allow Jesus to penetrate
And possess my whole being so
Completely that my life, too, may
Radiate His light and love to others. Amen.

Prayer for Those Who Have Lost a Child to Abortion

(Fr. Frank Pavone)

Lord of all Life,
You have entrusted us to the care of one another,
And called us to be one Body in Christ.
You call us to rejoice with those who rejoice,
And to weep with those who weep.
Hear our prayer today

For our brothers and sisters who have lost children to
   abortion.
Help us to understand
The pain that is in their hearts,
And to be a living sign to them
Of your welcome, your mercy, and your healing.
Help them to undergo with courage
The process of grief and the journey of healing.
Never allow them to feel alone;
Always refresh them with the presence of Your Spirit
And of their brothers and sisters in Christ.
Console them with the sure hope
That you love and care for their children.
Give them new strength,
That even while they grieve what they have lost,
They may look forward to all the good
That you still have in store for them.
Lord of healing and hope,
Give us all the forgiveness of our sins,
And the joy of your salvation.
We ask this in the name of Jesus the Lord. Amen.

Lovely Lady Dressed in Blue

(Unknown)

Lovely Lady dressed in blue
Teach me how to pray!
God was just your little boy,
Tell me what to say!
Did you lift Him up, sometimes,
Gently on your knee?
Did you sing to Him the way
Mother does to me?
Did you hold His hand at night?
Did you ever try
Telling stories of the world?
O! And did He cry?
Do you think He really cares
If I tell Him things—
Little things that happen? And
Do the Angels' wings
Make a noise? And can He hear
Me if I speak low?
Does He understand me now?
Tell me—for you know?
Lovely Lady dressed in blue—
Teach me how to pray!
God was just your little boy,
And you know the way. Amen.

Prayer Is the Breath of the Soul

(Cardinal Francis Xavier Nguyen Van Thuan)

Without prayer the soul suffocates.
Through prayer I live in you Lord.
I live in you as a baby in its mother's womb
with its breath united to hers
and its heart beating in rhythm with hers. . . .
Lord Jesus, you are my model.
The Gospel portrays you as praying
an entire night on the mountain.
You prayed before working your miracles,
before choosing your apostles,
and during the Last Supper.
You prayed as you sweat blood
in the Garden of Gethsemane;
you prayed during your agony on the cross.
You, the Incarnate Word,
prayed also with Scripture.
Your existence was one continuous prayer. Amen.

Closing Prayer of *Evangelium Vitae*
(Blessed Pope John Paul II)

O Mary,
bright dawn of the new world,
Mother of the living,
to you do we entrust the cause of life
Look down, O Mother,
upon the vast numbers
of babies not allowed to be born,
of the poor whose lives are made difficult,
of men and women
who are victims of brutal violence,
of the elderly and the sick killed
by indifference or out of misguided mercy.
Grant that all who believe in your Son
may proclaim the Gospel of life
with honesty and love
to the people of our time.

Obtain for them the grace
to accept that Gospel
as a gift ever new,
the joy of celebrating it with gratitude
throughout their lives
and the courage to bear witness to it
resolutely, in order to build,

together with all people of good will,
the civilization of truth and love,
to the praise and glory of God,
the Creator and lover of life. Amen.

Prayer for Our Nation (USA)

God Our Father, Giver of life,
we entrust the United States of America to your loving care.
You are the rock on which this nation was founded.
You alone are the true source
of our cherished rights
to life, liberty, and the pursuit of happiness.
Reclaim this land for your glory
and dwell among your people.
Send your Spirit to touch the hearts of our nation's leaders.
Open their minds
to the great worth of human life
and the responsibilities that accompany human
freedom. Remind your people that true happiness is
    rooted in seeking and doing your will.
Through the intercession of
Mary Immaculate, Patroness of our land,
grant us the courage to reject
the "culture of death."
Lead us into a new millennium of life.
We ask this through Christ our Lord. Amen.

Pope Francis Speaks to Mothers

In February, 2005, then-Cardinal Jorge Mario Bergoglio chose to celebrate the Mass for Holy Thursday in a maternity hospital in Buenos Aires, where he washed the feet of twelve expectant and new mothers. Before he washed their feet, he told them, "Some of you are holding your babies in your arms. Others of you are carrying them in your womb. All of you are women who have chosen life. I as a priest, am going to repeat the act of Jesus, and carry out a concrete act of service for women who have said yes to life. In washing your feet, I am washing those of all mothers, and of my mother, who felt me in her womb."